What to Say When You're Not Sorry Anymore

and other

Outtakes & Observations

**Verses for Women
by
Marjorie J. Scott**

ISBN: 1-4033-9067-3 (e-book)
ISBN: 1-4033-9068-1 (Paperback)

This book is printed on acid free paper.

1stBooks – rev. 12/24/02

Dedicated to Everywoman:

Those who have been there, done that, those who still have time, and especially to Lillian Cunningham whose Writer's Retreat at Windward Community College opens the door of imagination each month, with consummate skill.

These periodicals need to be acknowledged for choosing to publish the following poems which appear in this collection:

"Summer at Cross Lake"
    RAINBIRD, literary annual of
    U. of Hawai'i, Windward
    Community College (2001)

"Ann the Plain"
    TUCUMCARI LITERARY REVIEW (2000)

"Hitching Post In Amboy"
    PRAIRIE POETRY
    An E-zine

PROLOGUE

When I was very young I loved stories of
other peoples' lives; once I read a book called
"Up the Oronoco to Brazil" by Helen Follett and
another one called "Myself When Young a Boy
in Persia" and studied all the pictures of men
and women in embroidered costumes and big
winged hats in Alsace-Lorraine which is no
more, and was spellbound by myths of
Siegfried and Roland and gods of ancient
Greece, but the stories I remember best are
the ones about my family.

Grandma told stories in pinches and shakes
and spoonfuls and stirrings about how great
grandmother always carried a shotgun to the
chicken house because of the recent massacre
in New Ulm, and once she killed a rattlesnake
coiled on the sod floor of their log house
kitchen where baby grandpa was playing with
some new potatoes, so great gran planted her
highlaced shoe on the snake and chopped its
head off with a meat cleaver before it could
rise up and strike baby grandpa.

Grandpa bellowed his add-ons in whistles and
blurts and great guffaws about how great
grandfather strung the rattle on a leather
thong, and hung it 'round my grandpa's neck
when he was six and they had built a real
house near Albert Lea, with planked wood
floors and a heavy locking door between the
kitchen and the chicken yard, where the
rattlesnakes were all gone because of barn
cats and a bushy dog that growled, and you
didn't need a shotgun to collect the eggs.

Dad whipped out stories in snaps, and
aromatic pipe tobacco puffs about how he and
his brother wired an electric buzzer under the
fourth step felt pad of the narrow stairs up to
the loft, so they could sleep late on school days
and only get up when my stone-deaf grandad
started up the stairs with a heavy paddle in
case they weren't up yet, only they bargained
without grandma who found the buzzer and
removed it; my dad and uncle Ben learned
about getting up the hard way.

Mother stitched her story in pieces, pauses
and carefully worked seams about how she
was a tomboy who played baseball with the
Northeast boys who didn't know that one so
tiny could hit so hard, until she drove a fly
ball through a neighbor's parlor window and
grandma made her stick to her piano lessons
and she earned a Wurlitzer baby grand
playing piano in a Minneapolis store, so that
I grew up listening to her play Chopin, Haydn
and Grieg while I did my homework nearby.

My kitchen floor is gold-flecked tile squares.
The chicken I buy is frozen fast in plastic
trays. My alarm clock wakes me up with radio
news. I've never been to Brazil or Persia but
the German-French border which was Alsace-
Lorraine is flower boxed, quaint and cobbled,
and Greece is all marble ruins and olive oil,
unlike the fragrant dark German forests of the
myth gods, and sometimes when I'm writing
of the past, I hang the yellowed rattle on its
brittle thong around my neck for good luck.

What to Say When You're Not Sorry Anymore and
Other Outtakes and Observations

OUT TAKES

thoughts that got taken out of the action
…and shouldn't have

*Identify and acknowledge your own hidden agenda and
you'll find it easier to see someone else's.*

Jonathan Cainer
May 2001

Marjorie J. Scott

QUESTIONS

Is a cup enough to hold my thoughts, the
outpourings of my brain?

Is a jar that lids them down, the way to save
their essence, as if elixir or a precious potion?

Am I so inward turned to dream of substance
wishfully distilled that will live on in
generations still unborn?

A legacy to be discovered like an ancient ship
beneath a sea of churning memories biding
time, or soar in space to some future sphere?

Move on oh thoughts. Find your own sea to
sail, sky to fly, cup to sip or jar to lie buried in
timeless mystery.

In search of answers to the past, I am
compelled to dig deep into my history.

BIRTH

Pleasure and pain come with each other,
a matched pair, for who would know
the extent of pleasure without having
experienced the extremes of pain.

Who could feel the full physical glow
which comes from an infant's instant
smile, tiny arms that later clasp your neck
in an embrace of unconditional love.

Feel the final unremitting waves of pain
that baby foisted on your bloated body,
forcing it's passage to an independent life
outside the comfort of your womb.

Pleasure and pain come with each other,
the overture to instant joy and distant grief.

SMALL WORLD

So tiny in her crib
holding life at bay
until a future day
when lidded eyes will focus
when lips will turn to words
the gurgles, cries she makes
that bring two voices
to her side.

She hears a gentle
soothing sound
her source of food;
another deeper, sheltering
voice encloses her,
in time to come she'll learn to see
the vessel of her world
contains not one, but three.

PERSEID SHOWER

This night is filled with fireflies from space, an
awesome sight. We are amazed and question
how it all began beyond our womb of Co2 and
H2o and all the things that we don't know
about the universe.

A thousand years from now will planet Earth
return to dust, dispensing sparks called space
debris which folks like us will watch another
summer night from yards on distant planets in
another galaxy?

This night against the stenciled black of trees
and bushes by the fence, the dark is filled with
flitting fireflies, and little kids don't care about
the fate of stars, awed by magic bursts of light,
safe in their own backyards.

TEN AGAIN

I see my child sitting, head down, in the
old swing hung from the biggest low limb of
our maple tree. November's branches look
forlorn and awkward stripped of leaves, and
so does she, but she was

never awkward, she is smart, much sharper
than I ever was at ten, until today. What can
I say to stop the twisting turning thoughts
that has her out of balance on the swing she
twists and turns to tug my heart

off beat, apart. What can I do, or must I stay
away, let her find herself alone? Is ten
sufficient time to choose to own the troubles,
angers, losses of the grown? When I was
young and miserable I turned to candy bars.

Marjorie J. Scott

SUMMER AT CROSS LAKE

No shoes
It takes bare feet to creep across
the creaky cabin floor
before the birds awake,
escape into the silent
chilly dew of dawn.

No suit
It takes bare skin to slide into the lake
in secret rendezvous
surprising darting minnows
and a feeding bass
just as the goose bumps rise.

No more
It takes a child in distant past
to savor fear of snakes
beneath the porch, to bear the itching
rash that ivy leaves, and wear the heat
of sunburn like a badge.

RITE OF PASSAGE

Collections are the memories a child keeps
in closet, cupboard, pocket heaps, belongings
that are his or hers alone: a colored stone,
a key that has no lock, the springs and
inner workings of a broken clock.

It once was so in days of play before the mouse,
when outdoors held more action than the house,
when knowledge came from squirmy worms
and insect bites, when rites of passage came from
knees scraped raw, from tears for fights just lost,
or bully jeers wiped clean with cookies and
some milk, the fears erased when father's words
invoked self confidence.

A keystroke sets the pattern now,
book marked selected blames and shames
feed memory locked up behind a password
on a disk, collections hidden from reality,
a fertilizing dung for inner turmoil, guilt
to mushroom in the darkest kinds of games
without a guiding voice or hand to halt
the maims of anger, turn aside self-doubt.

Bring out the battles once again, the
punches, scrapes and body blows that
shape a boy into a man, that toughen hide
and goad the will to win; despite the world without
the rite of passage is within.

Marjorie J. Scott

ANNE THE PLAIN

How can you tell her that she's plain,
she knows you know and yet
will never hear you say wear red or
bleach your hair, or take the day.

Instead, you lead her in a dance and
teach her how to paint a sunrise on a
far-off hill, until her spirit fills her eyes
and stills her wanting heart for now.

Plain is not simple though, and soon
enough will come the day when one
enraptured by her soul and off'ring more
will take her heart and lead the way.

LESSONS

It is not love, it's lust, your
helium giggling and dream
dimmed eyes are lies, but
who can understand the truth
just turned fifteen.

It is not death, it's growth, when
you are left bereft, hormones
adrift, a natural rift in growing up,
but you can't bear to hear these words
just turned fifteen.

It is okay to sigh, to cry, to turn aside
when life seems cruel, tomorrow
you will start to drool at a new boy's
smile, and hog the phone for hours
because you are fifteen.

ALL GROWN UP

Once she danced, skipped,
grabbed at a passing butterfly,
her eager laughter the
tinkling bells of fairies
making music in my ears.

Once my day was brilliant
with the light that sparkled
at me from her bright young eyes,
an innocence more wise by far
than all the learning yet to come.

Some day I'll be the mentor to
another just like her, a time to play
grandmother in a way I hope
will be a copy of the special friend
my grandma was to me.

SNOT NOSED KID

Why does he turn to me, this snot nosed boy
almost a man with tales laced with "fuck" and "shit"
and girls not wearing underwear?

Where did he learn that confronting mother while she
held a kitchen knife to cut the roast was a clever ploy
to test response?

What does it take to prove that he's okay,
and so am I with what it takes for him to learn that I
can also be his friend?

When will he let me go as role model for the
woman he will wed, and when that day occurs am I
strong enough to let him go?

Who is this snot nosed kid that tries me so
that I, blind sided to the woman that I am
can not yet see the loving boy he is to me?

Marjorie J. Scott

TO A SON

Give it up, it's not love;
lust if you must, and
all men do, but soon enough
the passion ends.

Give it up, you're only 20
there's plenty of time, and
one to love for life, beyond
your heat's demands.

Give it up, find out first if you
can build a life to stand alone,
then only can you bear the
weight of wedding bands.

TO MY CHILD

Why do you have to die before I do?
        because I didn't want to know
        that you were gay.
Now you stay away.

How will I survive when you are gone?
        because I turn aside
        to keep my pride
In calling you my "son".

When sorrow wells, friends come by,
        the ones who sit by you for hours,
        who understand our troubled hearts
I hope you like the flowers.

Marjorie J. Scott

OVERHEARD: My Children's Tree

My limbs, shed of their growth crackle in the wind. My trunk thick and heavy now covers itself with lichen as if to hide its rough and mottled skin. The long roots of my life that no one remembers anymore but me still hold me to this earth, but now they lie cold and dormant, unvisited by small boys and their dogs, small giggling girls and their dolls. So long ago.

In the summer of my life they used to come, one at a time, to snuggle barely formed buttocks against my dried crotch, a tiny warm back pressed to my belly. One little boy in particular. He would stretch his legs out between my thick, gnarled thighs and rub the knot of my exposed and aging roots as if a magic lamp from which a genie would miraculously arise.

He would tell me his little secrets, his disappointments, his grief and his angers, knowing they would be safely hidden in the crevices of my bark. Summers came and summers went and he grew bigger as I grew older. In autumns, he would build brown houses on the ground with all my withered leaves; in winters, trim my lower barren limbs with tiny lights.

Too soon the spring arrived when he could no longer squeeze his body angles tight to mine. He brought a baseball. See, he said, tossing it straight up, trying to reach above me. See? I have a baseball now, I made the team, I have to go, and then, oh then, his tiny sister broke his grasp and clasped her arms part way around my trunk and claimed me for her tree, so long ago.

A WOMAN'S POETRY

A woman's poetry
　　　　is everything she doesn't say
　　　　steadied by a prayer
　　　　when she is sad or longing,
　　　　hurt or angered

A woman's poetry
　　　　is star bright in her eyes,
　　　　the fan of smile lines
　　　　grown beside from the pleasures
　　　　of her day

A woman's poetry
　　　　is hugging close her child
　　　　smoothing stress and worry
　　　　from a weary neck, giving
　　　　even when she's tired

A woman's poetry
　　　　is every day an inner voice
　　　　that incubates her love,
　　　　bursts forth in scents and tastes
　　　　on family dinner plates

A woman's poetry
　　　　is how she lives her life,
　　　　the static of the world tuned out
　　　　by angels guarding constantly
　　　　within her soul

SEDUCTRESS

I wear no fragrance but the scent of
cinnamon dusted on buttered toast,
garlic added to spaghetti sauce, onion,
dill and lemon juice, the fragrant breath
of Cabernet; I cannot be ignored.

I wear no polish but the sheen of
olive oil on my hands from
rubbing Russets before they bake, the
plump breast of chicken before it roasts;
I enrapture men.

No kiss is sweeter than a second
helping, no hug warmer than a refilled
glass, an emptied plate,
no love is more enduring than men for
their meal; I satisfy their appetites.

THE FRIENDLIEST GIFT

She's 88? How can that be? I cannot contemplate the
year when I display the patina of her age, no sage to
tell me how to achieve the brightness of her eyes or
wisdom of her outlook on the ways of sister, nieces,
nephews, friends, it all depends on how I fit the pieces
of my history into the puzzle of my life.

No strife afflicts this cheerful aunt that cannot be
endured and put behind, a mind that traps the present
in a smile, an easy question of a stranger, all the while
intent on who they are, by far the friendliest gift to
offer anyone: a probing curiosity defying fears of those
who seek her ears to fill with troubles of their own.

Alone she lives, her needs fulfilled by those she's
bonded to, thus I renew my spirit to go on, stand
straighter in my willingness to dream; she seems to
understand, her brand of courage rare these days, her
praise an energy, a spark that gives me pause to pity
those who've lost the way to make their mark.

Marjorie J. Scott

A CHAIR TO FILL

He's gone, and yet he fills her daily life with his
routine, his chair stands where it always will, across
the room from hers, she still turns on the set to watch
his favorite sports and TV Soap.

He is no longer here, despite his family pictures on the
wall, his room contains her desk and books where once
he stored his life in drawers, on shelves and hooks,
his fishing rods and tackle told it all.

His chosen cereal stands beside her own, material for
memories should she so choose, a food link to their
fifty years; no tears remain, it is a natural time to
gain release from chains of daily stress.

He left a chair to fill and so we do, restoring balance to
replace the strife that loss of sight and hearing brought
to bear upon a wife who long ago arranged her days
to work with church and friends.

She is the stalwart one who bakes the cakes and
visits with the sick, she takes her aging aches in
daily steps that set a goal for me to persevere: to
fill my chair of life to come with empathy.

COMING OUT

He told me things I didn't know how to hear
yet hearing brought us closer than before
and gave me trust I never knew I had
to be myself.

I languaged thoughts I never shared
with anyone 'til now, in space made safe
for speaking; by his gift I love him more
for opening my heart.

Proud he can be of who he says he is,
his courage coming out so late a challenge to
the mask I choose to wear, heroics do not fit
to validate my deeds.

While I abjure discovery of myself, my needs
contained like precious gems held far apart
from curious gaze, I now accept my straighter ways
to live this woman's life.

HEROES

There are no heroes in her life,
too tall an order to bring out
the charming prince in husband
weary, angry, still intent on
problems of his day, stone deaf
to rumblings of a wife who
struggles silent with her discontent.

Bent on a beer and smells of dinner
missing while she rests, herself a
human being not a kitchen wench
born to serve, he has the nerve to ask
"when's dinner?" when she wants
to hear "how was your day?" though
she may choose to simply say "ok".

She wishes now that she'd been born
her daughter or granddaughter's age, a
present time when loving pairs share
kitchen chores as well as bed; trusting
in each other's constancy they listen to the
story of each other's day, bravely facing
perils of their honesty instead.

WHAT TOOK SO LONG?

What took so long to see
beyond the dreams we had,
to hear the clocks that ticked within
each on a different time zone of
our past and future sin that formed
the mind warped vista of our lives,
a fun house mirror designed for
laughs seducing us instead to
aching inner tears for tossing out
the good times in the trash?

We took too long to look beyond the
need we thought we had to pair,
to pare away the shells of emptiness
we thought we had from living singly,
needing laughter, needing warmth,
wanting other ears to hear us speak
when there were none, forgetting that no
matter who we are, each is alone
to build a universe of love – or not.

Marjorie J. Scott

SOUL MATE

Your body's missing from my bed and
it's okay, we use our phone calls to
convey impassioned underpinnings
of remembered heat too dangerous now
too complex to compete with age and
AIDS and years of marriage in between.

The time away though lean has held our
love secure, safe from the world's fear, I hear
your voice, the words we never need to say
that warm my life, restore a gentler me
connected to your heart and soul, whole and
happy to have had those years with you.

MESS UP

cobwebs of my past
across the corner of my mind
obscured my sight
gone blind with mess

I was too tangled with beliefs
to confess an earthly need to be
supportable I thought,
when what I really ought
was to look inside of me

to see a crowd of strangers
standing by, to hear their cry
"don't stop … you're safe …
we'll catch you if you fall"
and get that it was perfect
just to Be. Thank you, all.

Marjorie J. Scott

GOSSIP

Fly in the face of gossip
flap past raised eyebrows
and pursed lips, soar high,
silent far above the crowd
in your nighttime forays,
stay watchful for stray cats that
hiss at your daytime ventures,
your private life is your own.

If you keep still about your
loving, your lusting, your
secret nests, protect your passions
behind a cooler image that
the public sees, speak straight
and true but softly, then you will
glow like iridescent feathers
caught in sunlight.

Let them gossip about that.

CLUMPS OF SILENCE

Small angers, hurts and disappointments
coiled like sleeping cats in clumps of silence
breathing quietly to stay alive and safe
until danger passes in the lightness of time.

Years have worn away embarrassment
from speaking up to startled looks, arched
eyebrows, eyes turned aside from hearing
words from murky corners of the mind.

Disappearing competition, mistrust, derision
born of jealousy, the threat of lost control
concerns no more, no hidden scores to settle
hiding out; maturity uncoils the ropes that
bind a tongue, revealing woman.

Marjorie J. Scott

TIME TO SPEAK

Take me there to where it doesn't hurt,
where loving dwells and swells
this life today, where I can play
in swirling liquid love winked gold by
sun, undone by thoughts pedestrian.

Take me there in leaps and loping lines
of prose upon the page, coursing rivers
of poesy, cutting through the pain of
living in this world again, a dismal dot
of dust swelled up of insignificant
interludes of self absorbing lust.

Take me there to where I might have
been implanted with your seed;
not heeding who I really am, I chose to
go alone through trial when all the
while I could have followed where you
led in passion's richer pastures.

What to Say When You're Not Sorry Anymore and
Other Outtakes and Observations

Be for me today what I have not yet
been, a wise and caring visitor to places
of my life to set them right in story,
glory in your celestial presence the
ground from which I'm rudely torn.

Take me there oh godhead of my birth
while there's still time for me to speak
wantonly, crudely and most of all
with passion and with mirth.

Marjorie J. Scott

CONFESSION TO MY MUSE

I must confess that to write for myself
is to write for a stranger,
one who enters without knocking,
interrupts what I am doing,
forces me to write as if my pen were
a gun at my head, then disappears
mid-line leaving me instead with
aching eyes, clenched throat, gasping
for breath, as if on my knees before
the Cross pleading release, forgive,
heal my beaten brain.

Your sudden witchery dams my mind
with clumps of junk, the flow of poesy
dried up, no single line attracted to my
silent pen I am reduced to nothing,
drawn out, exposed, naked, the glowing
words all gone as I lie broken clay,
value lost, tossed aside while the splintered
shell of what I was spills jagged chunks
across this page of pleas and prayers,
confessions I would never make if sane.

I am lost again to the stranger
that I am when you desert me.

MORNING PRAYER

I pray at the altar of my consciousness
that it may be
 free of fear,
 clear of grief,
 void of anger
and filled with only that passion which,
with soft voice and gentle touch
 nurtures children,
 nurses the wounded,
 protects the helpless and infirm;
most difficult of all, I pray within my
soul that I may
 give myself up to the will of the god
 we all presume,
who hearing what remains unspoken
will grant my surrender to a wiser love

Marjorie J. Scott

WHAT TO SAY WHEN YOU'RE NOT SORRY ANYMORE

fool to speak
wise to shut up,
or
is it the reverse?

So absolutely good is truth,
truth never hurts the teller.
Robert Browning
"Fifine at the Fair" (1872)

Marjorie J. Scott

MIRROR, MIRROR

Divine
devious
doesn't matter
mirrors lie
you cannot envision
who you need to be
by staring at your eyes,
they don't reflect the
person that you
truly are.

Makeup mars,
glitter gratifies
never you behind
your mask, just
the face you've
made to hide a
haunted
hidden
held back
gaze.

Get real for once
behind that painted maze.

IT DOESN'T MATTER

Once I did not know
the words to say to you
to stop the hurting
we hurled off point,
fouling each other's day,
no way to bring a halt
to stinging taunts, your
dismissal of my way
to cope with living
your life, not mine,
well fine,
this time I know exactly
what to say:
It doesn't matter anymore
in any way.

HONEYMOON

Tears you shed so freely over past imagined hurt
you wanted me to share and I could not. I had
my own pain buried deep in zipped up pockets
of my life, impervious to empathy.

You had good reason to repeat your plea for me
to love whom you loved just because you did, and
so I hid from you my lack of neediness to be
attached by mother, father dependency.

Viewing it now, it was our undoing.

Marjorie J. Scott

QUARREL

All over but the shouting? Not true.
The shouting started it, you lost control;
I blew you off. Once more our silence shouts,
I'm on a roll. Please just shut up and go.

All over but the crying? Yes, if that's what
you would like to do. Me? Quietly
recalling better times of fun and laughter,
I can forget our discontents, can you?

IN THIS LIFETIME

In this lifetime
my body is earthbound
my head is in the clouds
take me this way,
thoroughly
completely
often
or leave me alone
to play my passion out
with greater gods.

Marjorie J. Scott

FLAMED OUT

Why must you always talk
me me me
never listen
you you,
your voice
buzzing my brain
stinging my passion into fury
fired so high
my love burns to ashes
on your tongue
talking to yourself

WINTER STORM

grinding cold
chipping at my jaw
watering my eyes
chattering my teeth,
you wind whip
words of icy anger
blue lipping my face,
chilling chunks of love,

in cold disregard you miss
my own winter storm
moving in on you
so fiercely that
your tormenting tongue
freezes solid in your mouth,
prey to my chisel sculpting
Ice Man of the Month.

Marjorie J. Scott

HEAVY?

The sofa is heavy
two bulging, heaving
men-worth to move its
butt cushioned frame,
look out, don't scrape
the walls, don't hit
the door jamb.

Heavy, no you're
not bulging, not heaving
not butt pushing
my throbbing cushions,
not anywhere near scraping
my hot pulsing walls, not
even hitting my jammed up
door so that it screeches my
body out over my swollen,
searching tongue.

Stick to sofas.

NIGHT WORDS

Night words rumble
like a belly full of gas
revenging gluttonous sex
disguised as love,
habituated coupling
out of tune, so soon
a bloated bubble of the past
explodes the dream of continence
in bursts of hurt

WHAT WOULD HAPPEN IF…

…I shared my real thoughts with you,
instead of "never mind I'm fine" or "I
can't stay" or feigned sleepiness?

…I said things other than "let's eat out",
"when's our tee time?", "the bathroom's
free now", or said nothing at all?

…I showed you how I really feel by
yawning in the face of your complaints,
showed anger when you wouldn't help?

…I told you how the things I really care
about are goals I set before we met,
what would happen then?

I am me, a person you can never see for
expecting me to be a different woman,
one that I will never know. Tell me lover,
if you can, what happens now?

I WILL BELIEVE YOU WHEN YOU LIE

I will believe you when you lie
for then I'll know there's guilt behind
that pitiful "truth is" posturing
    silly peabrained peacock

I will trust you when you cheat
for now I know your stockinged tread
approach at midnight with a shaky step
    silly would-be womanizer

I will love you when you hate
that I have found you out and let
you get away with offering flowers
    silly aging cavalier

I 'll stay your wife no matter what
because I tryst sometimes myself and
you will never ever know
    silly cuckold cocksman

Marjorie J. Scott

MOVING OUT

Your heart beats I know because
I watch you breathe, but do you cry?
I've never seen your eyes grow
moist with hurt or loss, you want me
to believe you are the stoic boss of your
emotions, but you're not,
you're vulnerable just like me.

When you can let me see that you are
human too, I may come back. For now, I
choose to move from under your silence
where I am free to laugh out loud, to
stomp and yell in anger, wail in pain, and
most of all hear passionate moans and
shouts from you in my embrace.

YOUR STORY

What is your story?
you do not speak,
words rumbling inside,
are you afraid they
will leak out if you
open your mouth?

I've read your script
same old commas, periods
in a row, with
nothing in between.
I'll take my leave while
silence still becomes you.

Marjorie J. Scott

TOO LATE

All the things I never said are past
and gone too late; if all the ways I am today
I had been then would we have turned
a page beyond my want for you to hear me
spill my day like boiling oil at your feet?

Would you have turned my heat to
soothing balm –any lie would do –
to glue us back together, whether or not
I would have stayed to weather
another of our storms?

Too late
the things I never said
could not be said 'til now;
the season of our ripening fruit
has come and gone.

WE LOVED

We loved
and loved
and loved
and thought we did
    until you went to
    squeeze the juice
    and brew the coffee
and I went back to sleep
and never heard you leave
and never knew this was the end
    until right now
and it is night again
and I am back in bed
and it's all mine
and life is fine.

ENDING

I know no death except the death of love;
a flower blossom dies, I do not mourn,
another will be born in its place.

I know only loss, which is not the end
of living, but rather the beginning of
emptiness, a space to be filled up again.

I did not lose you; what I thought I lost
was the fullness of my time only to find
that you simply ceased to exist for me.

GREAT WALL

When your love for me
finally died,
I buried it
where it lay,
safely outside
the wall of my heart.

Others grope
in hope of what they think
they'll find
but never will,
my heart is sealed forever
from your hurt.

Marjorie J. Scott

LATE NEWS

My dear, congrats, you made it through,
we two were never meant to share more
than some laughs, the air in which
we danced and golfed, how wise to turn us off.

My dear, much praise, you raised the ante
on how two should be attached, I am amazed
at how mismatched we were, and still
appeared the perfect couple to our friends.

My dear, be very clear about the nature of
this note: it is not meant to make amends;
in case we ever meet as friends you need to
  know the score:
  I'm just not sorry anymore.

'HELLO' IS FINE

'Hello is fine
since we are unlocked from love,
you going your way, me going mine
'Hello is fine.

'Hello' is fine
to break the strain of holding guilt
or pain that separates us like a battle line
'Hello' is fine

'Hello' is fine
for being your friend, or acquaintance
if you prefer, you being mine
'Hello' is fine.

And so 'hello'
and 'hello' again some time,
'hello', just 'hello' will do,
'Hello is fine.

YOUR FRIENDS

Once we were a family,
I bore your name
shared your bed
welcomed to our home
       your friends

In air, on ground, at sea
we chose to travel far
and live in constant company
of those who were
       your friends

I cried a lot for all
the things you didn't share,
my needs, my wants my dreams
did not include
       your friends

What to Say When You're Not Sorry Anymore and
Other Outtakes and Observations

We parted then
the difference too wide to breach
between our lifestyle goals,
I reached to make
        new friends

The years 'til now are filled with
memories of private hope and
growing kids, the rope of time
still binds the years among
        your friends

You brought me pictures of your kids
grown tall with children of their own
and quickly squeezed my hand to
let me know the wonder of it all:
        I'm still your friend.

Marjorie J. Scott

OBSERVATIONS

One must live first, before one can speak with any credibility about living.

> *Too soon old,*
> *Too late smart*
> > *old saying*

Marjorie J. Scott

LEGENDS OF THE PAST

I live the legends of my past
in sunlight dreams that
softly drift on breezes
free from dour clouds,
allow at last selected joys and
angers, fears and grief their
pictures in the brief still hours
an aging time allows.

Some tattered worn and faded,
others bright and clear to view,
a quilt of life to pull around
my day, to warm the leisure play
of classic movies depict the way
I used to be, and see that these are
merely legends now to keep intact
or throw away.

A WOMAN AGING

Consider this:
age does not "advance", you do;
you can charge right through
the years and leave them breathless
if you've kept a vigorous mind
unkind to protests from the
young who urge "slow down".

Abound in morning walks and
stretches, a nap, a vitamin or two,
the night is made for play, though
that may be an evening of TV,
who knows but you the solace found
in tales of aged celebrities whose lives
have long since passed from view.

"Need help?" they ask, of course,
but not the way they mean,
the need of woman aging is a man
to make her smile, show off
the laugh lines 'round her eyes
and all the while hold her years
a special prize for him alone.

When none's around, you make the
best of traveling in a younger set
who hold no mirrors to your past,
but let you be a mystery of wisdom
to imbibe in savory sips, a treasure
held in secret like a costly vintage wine,
consider aging as a precious gift.

Marjorie J. Scott

WHO AM I?

Am I a Sophisticate,
who pillowed and blanketed
absorbs the articulations of
the apparently literate
over morning coffee in bed?

Am I a Culinaire
who orders a la carte
in French the most exquisite
from the curly cursived list
unpriced, in flickering candlelight?

Am I not, instead
Eternal Dreamer savoring
every pretense wealth can buy
to salve my guilty conscience
for a half-committed life?

Call me what you will,
to be Alive at all is still a thrill.

LIGHT LUNCH

We face across a tabletop wiped clean,
and study menus to escape the throb
between the thighs, adjust our eyes to
hide our hearts.

We talk around confessions barely
hidden, choosing words far from the
sighs of youthful heat, too late surprised
by sexual longings, we retreat.

You order cake and ice cream
I can't have, I ask for salad greens and
very cold iced tea.

Marjorie J. Scott

TIME OF YOUR LIFE

The time you have is infinite like nature for
the tree that leaps a foot each year fed by
persistent tropic rains, sun so warm that
flowers bloom the whole year round, no
change of season dares to show itself.

In all the time there is hold close the giant
portion for yourselves to warm your days,
turn up the lips that puff your aging cheeks
and add a telltale line of smile beside each
eye which begs response.

With tears of joy accept each life-filled
minute of the newborn day, and pray that
Spirit has its way with you; like dew caressing
meadows of your mind, quench thirst for
living in a burst of laughter from a child.

OH SENTIENT CAT

Curved and comforting,
offering encouragement,
sometimes hissing,
casting me away from dreams
until suddenly swung high
into the dawn on loud meows,
I am thrust from rolling billows
of my sleep into the mind
game trappings of mortality
in which I spend a lifetime every
day expending my identity,
because the hungry cat that
owns me wants my energy.

Marjorie J. Scott

THE CHILD OF MY OLD AGE

My child has whiskers, he's all I have,
instead of cries, he meows or leaves the house without
a word; ordinary cats may do, but he's not ordinary.

My child with whiskers wants no milk and won't drink
water either, but growls and paws the table like a litter
box unless there's gravy in his food.

My child who's all I have complains and sulks when
doors are closed between us, then finds a space behind
my legs to sleep the night content.

This child of my old age will never leave because I tell
him "no" or "bad" or "stay" when he won't do exactly
what I want, he knows in time he'll get his way.

FUTURELAFF

We, like frantic crabs forever
clawing at each other's heads
to reach an edge that isn't there,
despair the world we've made of pain
back into life without the will
to do what visioning requires.

An impassioned few will take the leap
in present time to keep a promise made
before descending through the chaos
known as "birth", and out of mind
the Powers That Be will see and
hold their sides in blissed-out mirth

What ho!
the Heavens are finally moving Earth!

Marjorie J. Scott

SENSEI

Too late his words, I say
too many years cementing
fixed ideas to my memory banks
to build a fortress around
my consciousness.

Too late his chant, I say
too many prayers between myself
and Taoist ways to soar into
an altered universe
of mindlessness.

Too late, despite my plea to
feel the softness of an angel's wings
wrapped safe around my palmistry,
a doorway opening wide belies
my senselessness.

SOME WINE HAS SOURED

Of all the vintage years of pressed and bottled
memories, aromas, tastes that bring on smiles,
wistfulness, and tears, some wine of mine has
soured, aged by strife.

We are not as we were before the myrrh
set in, we risk more candor than we ever did
to start, the truth of sweet and sour combined
is difficult to find in heady youth.

For all of that, the vinegar remains the tart
mother in the messages poured on budding
sprouts that peaks their flavor, stimulates their
inborn power and healthy growth.

Marjorie J. Scott

THE OCEAN DOESN'T CARE

The ocean doesn't care,
that it was me before I was,
ten thousand years ago,
before the edge of all the time we know;
me in the sea
pulsing,
pulsing
deep beneath the sleep of ages,
wave after
wave after
wave of time,
wearing down the edges all around until we came
aground, washed up forever from her greatness,
from where it all began and then will end.

The ocean mother of us all
doesn't care to bear the burden of our sins,
her time will come again when we are naught.

THE VOICE OF FAMILY

The voice of family a Siren's call
    across the years that turns my ears away
    from living independent day-to-day
that makes a sham of homegrown homily:
    you didn't hear…
    how could she have…
    I told them not…
forgotten
    in a single smile, a hug and "welcome!"
years of building who I am from virgin clay
    that seldom bore a hint of blooded root,
my history moot.

    That luring witch, that temptress' song
    seducing me from emptiness
    with greetings warm and filled with love
    to break my heart for when I must depart alone
    a Self enticed by history told around
    and filled with memories of a childhood shared,
    impaired by what can never be

I leave now
changed and torn away
    from all I've said I was
    because I never chose
    the closeness bound inside
from pride of owning family.

Marjorie J. Scott

YOU'LL HAVE TO WAIT

Oh no, not yet,
it's not time to turn in
this trunk of life,
       see?
it's not full yet.

Here's a corner needs a hug,
and here, down here,
       peer way down,
that empty space needs
filling with a memory
too long alone, and there
       reach in there
between those layers
a humped up pain needs healing
to relax again.

What to Say When You're Not Sorry Anymore and
Other Outtakes and Observations

I am undone
so many little holes alive with
thoughts ready to be spoken,
broken down, laid to rest
      by me, not you
can't you see this whole top layer
wants using up?

Slow down, you'll have to wait,
I'm not yet ready to be blessed
a final time, you've missed the point
of what aliveness is about,
      go
      close the door
      wait quietly
there's more to do, to have, to be,
before I say farewell to me.

Marjorie J. Scott

WHAT IF?

What if
this is what it is to be
closer to an ending than a beginning,
to know your next Big Project will be
carried on by someone else,
to give up control of tomorrows no longer
the children of your imagination?

What if
this is how it is to plan days
tightly full of nothing very urgent so that
if tomorrow never comes at least today
is filled with endless busyness,
booked to look proud and productive,
to whoever comes to give it all away?

What if
you cannot be your age,
your mind is stuck on 40, 50, maybe younger,
you cheer for what enthuses you,
you rant and rave in desperation at delays
in projects you alone have filled
with meaningless meaning?

What if
it never mattered who you were
until now when ending is so near and
strangers know your name and smile
in passing on the street so that you move
bewildered in a milieu on a different path
than you recall?

What if
the laugh's on you and no one cares
at all the year depicted in the lines
that grid your face, never focus on the
thickened waist you try to hide, see instead
the bright aliveness in your eyes that's always there
because it's where you live.

Marjorie J. Scott

ANOTHER VIEW

A tin of aspirin
to you all
who drive your grandkids
to the mall,
I never do.

A badge of courage
is what you rate
who play Nintendo with
a child of eight,
I'm awed by you.

My game plan
is of a sweeter sort,
we play hide and seek,
and bake some cookies
for our sport.

CLEANING HOUSE

I vacuum up the tiny bits
of past that litter and disturb the
tranquil patterned carpet of
my life, so I can tread an ordered
path from here to there.

So where did this debris exist
in all my modest history, that
should insist a grubby presence of
itself upon my peaceful life to
force this labored work?

What quirk, what strife does it
remind, of past misdeeds or troubled
mind to take away my afternoon
to cook and sew and maybe find
a quiet hour with a book?

I sigh, and caring less, I set about to
trash this mess with vigor and
determined mind; the laugh's on me,
it's just the crumbs and garden dirt
my grandkids left behind.

Marjorie J. Scott

Tuesday's Come and Gone

Tuesday's come and gone
like Christmas on its final day,
a string of hugs packed
carefully away behind my eyes
against the emptiness of time.

Tuesday's come and gone
the high clear giggles drowned
by talking heads, a beggar's poor resort;
a TV dinner's taste destroys the
last sweet breathless kiss
and I am left a Grandma long
divorced from playful innocence.

I am left to ponder through
the days the ways that Tuesdays
have their hold, small arms
clung tight around my leg,
a child seeking root in tales retold
of how I lived when I was four,
of how their father spent his youth.

The truth is that
I dwell benign within myself
amid the shadows of my week
to hide the secret of its legacy
that Tuesdays pass too fast at 63.

I AM NOT LATE

I am not late, not dead to time,
just aging in a space of deeds
too thin and thoughts too fat
to concentrate or fit the pace.

Not former, in this
latter day of email push and
words too readily keyed to
grace a page with meaning.

Not waiting for, not slow
nor lacking energy, not stopped,
not forgetting, I'm right on time
just minutes behind a lazy clock.

Marjorie J. Scott

PERHAPS I 'VE GROWN TOO DULL

Perhaps I've grown too dull,
I cry at death and push back shadows
of my own approaching time
with inner chill and outward stands
among my friends.
    But don't we all protest The End
    as if our serving work were armored plate
    defying "fate" — whatever that is?

I smile at puppies, kittens, babies
stretching limbs in toppling play,
sponges of innocence sopping up
minutiae for the seeding of their lives,
and blow the dust from mine.
    But don't we all decry our aging
    impotence as if our fatless food and
    exercise could now restore a supple mind?

I'm not Millennium "news".
Of course I could restructure growing up
on more dysfunctional lines to win
acceptance on the street, and paint myself
a woman filled with angry pain.
      But few are left to care about a time that glued
      a sisterhood to silence, unbidden oracles to the
      politics of public outcry.

Perhaps we've all grown dulled by years of
coping with the twisted fibers of our histories,
brilliance muted in the malleable fabrics shaped
to fit another age when honeyed sweetness
in our cup was prize enough for being alive.
      But who of us does not seize love
      to heal the young who choose denial
      of the scars ahead and wind up dead?

Marjorie J. Scott

TREES OF HER LIFE

She ran until a root
surprised her and she tripped,
cried "Mommy" once, and
crawled up on a stump to dry
her tears and scold the forest floor
when she was four.

Her name was not the one
carved in the heart with his
along the path to school, it made
her mean; she kicked the ancient
trunk, bark fell at her feet
when she was just thirteen.

Imprisoned in cement they
stood, a guardian row of victim
trees, leaves hiding toxic sky and
serving eager dogs along the
run she took each day to work
when she was twenty-one.

Beneath the canopy of green that
roofed her deck, she thanked whatever
stars kept her so long alive,
a yellowed leaf dropped in her lap,
she blessed it with a kiss
when she was sixty-five.

They spread a dappled shade upon
the granite plaque that bears her
name beneath them on the grassy
floor, forgotten now except by
they who shared her soul,
until she died at ninety-four.

Marjorie J. Scott

GRANDMA'S ROOM REMEMBERED

I enter quietly
this sanctuary from reality
from 2+2's and 4x4's, from
ugly nasties of a childhood fight
from colds and flus
and a chill gray sleety
winter day.

Drop away my cares, guarded as
I am by giant chests
that live against these walls
veneered and matching,
polished to a glowing shine,
for me a spacious palace
in this tiny room, filled up with
treasures from another world
not mine.

What to Say When You're Not Sorry Anymore and
Other Outtakes and Observations

Slip past the
brass strapped cedar chest
against the narrow bed
instead sit cross-legged on the
tulip garden quilt and hear the rise of
iron rusty heat in gurgling hiss compete with
voices from the domed chromed radio.

Pursue a special time of
let's pretend
a secret life within a woman's
world of joy and sorrow dramatized
in fifteen minute plots of sweet soprano
and rich bass tones between the cake flour,
soaps and aspirin.

Marjorie J. Scott

Enthroned she sits
my Grandma in her
laced-up shoes, worn as
the upholstery of her stool
and chair, hair waved just so
above her steel-rimmed eyes.

She is wise to my escape
to seek the secrets of her feminine
mystique in crystal stoppered
drafts of luscious scent
and puffs of peachy powders in
her dresser drawers.

I live for hours in
pearl ropes and jeweled brooches
lifted slowly from their satin cells,
soft woolen scarves and
fringy silken shawls
adorn my back transforming
me to movie queen.

Atop the pink and green
of patchwork tulips
stitched by her just so,
imagine lives of
long dead relatives from
sepia photos of their
hourglass gowns and collar chokes,
in padded albums from a special box,
and enter through my Grandma's
tales of mom and dad
the days before my life.

When dinnertime arrives
and Mother calls us down,
a different little girl will
kiss her grandma's cheek and
put away the fantasy of me in
times from which I came,
all perfumed, powdered in a
past of lace with velvet ribbon trim,
to face less grim the next day
of my childhood.

Marjorie J. Scott

HITCHING POST IN AMBOY

Cold, old stone post with rusted iron ring
    a monument to life that is no more,
    a curbside sentry lone and gray,
    a silent ghost to family history.

The house is gone, the icehouse and the
outhouse too, where once a dozen feet
beat past; just grass where I recall a big oak
door, and deer with giant antlers etched
in frosted glass; just grass where once
I rocked a creaking front porch swing,
drank icy water from the kitchen pump.

Across the street the mourning doves still
coo. (The church bell rang the same when I
was four); somewhere I hear my aunts and
uncles laugh, see sweet corn bubbling on the
wood fire stove, smell peaches churning cold
in thick, sweet cream, and Granddad's house
is mine and safe once more.

WHERE AM I?

where am I
beyond this speck of sentient dust
with mobile facial hole that
swallows in or spits out
a garble of garbage called
"words"
of what it doesn't know and
makes believe it does.

where am I
behind this noisome facile tongue holding back a
cosmos pulsing hot with "I" who am where,
who came from where,
and shaped where within,
from particles of dust
unexplained.

where am I
before the sucking into blackness,
or after form too tightly fit to understand the spiraling
band
that repeats the pulse electric of
the universe unknown
where I am naught.

Marjorie J. Scott

THEY REST IN PEACE

We pinch dead blossoms from
petunia plants that grow around
the granite slab where B. and M.
rest quietly, the well-trimmed
slope of trees much taller now
than in the years when they passed on.

Across the curving auto path
another grassy slope with plates
of brass to mark the aunts and uncles
side by side who once skyscraped
above our baby heads, now resting
far below our memoried gaze.

Upon an older rise a monument
whose chiseled name was once well
known among the City's peers,
some sixty years ago I met his twinkling
eyes with childish glee at carpet games
he played with me.

In dignity his stone-carved presence
stands surrounded by the family that
was his, their names familiar from
my grandma's tales entwined with
mine, too young to know the way
to seek their history.

Below the Chapel's marbled floor
I find at last my grandpa, grandma and
an aunt whose name I bear,
their waking days are done and yet
in captioned album photos that I keep
deep run the roots entwined with mine.

Securing their remembrance
in prayer I thank them for release,
their rest divinely guarded in this
peaceful lake view place,
I now find solace in their sleep;
my history is safe, they rest in peace.

Marjorie J. Scott

AGES OF DELUSION

Aging makes me angry
     not at time wasted
        (it never is)
     not at time left
        (I have 24/7)
     not at time past
        (I have great stories)

I'm angry at the aging
     who mewl and complain
        like colicky babes
     who shun the world
        like victims of abuse
     who flaunt their years
        like medaled heroes

Aging is a wondrous time
of hours to remember
(the house can wait)
of naps whenever I want
(the body needs its sleep)
of exercise and vitamins
(the brain requires support)

Aging is a mentoring time
to challenge angry youth
to flex the muscles of the mind
to find the falsehoods of collusion;
the fields of life are mined
with ages of delusion
not with Truth.

Marjorie J. Scott

LATTER DAYS

Stranded
in the middle of this soft blue bed
the color warm, insuring calm they say
within this shrunken form,
her eyes fill with resentment for
becoming helpless prey, as smiling
they leave her in another's care
to dream of life that used to be.

Stranded
too far above the tile
for easy purchase by old feet
itching to walk the halls awhile
for folks to meet, for things to do,
she rings, and hears them starched
and squishing to seat her
stiffness by a window with a view.

Stranded
by time and temper
to be in another's keep,
patronized by strangers
and their cheery bleep,
in voiceless anger at
the loneliness they bring,
she shuts them out by feigning sleep.

Stranded?
She will strand them all, refuse their
food and flowers, leave them
wordless, use the hours to write a
diary that her grandson brought, for he
is stranded too, between the age of need
and being needed,
needy for this prisoner's end time view.

Intent, he reads her shaky lines and
turns to hide a rueful smile at how
his grandma's life is out of phase,
with tenderness he kisses her,
tucks candy in her hand, a secret treat,
escapes her fate on springy steps,
the soul mate of her latter days
free now, her legacy to him complete.

Marjorie J. Scott

ETERNAL DEADLINE

No glass of sand
nor timer's click
can hold it back,
fast, slow, dizzy or
in sleep, we move to
meet the ending
which our inner clocks will use.

The drummer's beat
rolls on to force
my season in the sun,
despite my pleas
the count to deadline
has begun; time is -
it's man who marches on.

VIGIL

Soon sleep will come, you will escape again beyond the sight of life you show to me. Longer now the shriveling away, or so it seems as other stresses press us down. Every light powered noon before the planet starts to tilt you leave. Do you fly or float or merely lie a rubbled heap too stressed to stay? You've never said, and I've never asked you why.

I'll sit here waiting nonetheless until those parchment lids sweep up revealing less than when they hid your soul from me. You smile from the corners of your face and find my eyes. My wordless nod responds, for after all the days of going out, our silence speaks the one thing left to say: will tomorrow be the day you choose to die?

Marjorie J. Scott

THOUGHTS ON A SUDDEN PASSING

We cannot know the hour of our demise
nor should it be a care, instead the minutes
of each day should wear our purest Self
like skin scrubbed clean of wanting more,
a seamless shell that holds and molds
the who we are whom others see.

Soft edges form as faces fade and
legends stretch to lay a claim to persons
that we hardly were; work then to weave
the carpet of our lives in colors that insure
our truer history will remain, that memories
of how we lived will be their gain.

SOME FRIENDS ARE GONE

I have no fear of what's
to come, for what could
be more fun than meeting
once again in spirit space.

We'll share the grace of love
that we forsook along the path
of life each took that changed a
body over time and lined a face.

They did not pass, they push up
grass as Grandma used to say;
in moments quiet, they speak to
to me in mind, and

I'm surprised to find myself
growing softer wrinkles in my skin,
ending each day with a gentler view;
aging is most kind.

Marjorie J. Scott

GRIEVING TIME

Cascade from heaven in
noisy splashing froth
as if the heart that
holds your sorrow were a
never ending source of rain,
your tears a waterfall of
such awesome power
I wait quiet, wrapped in
your mist, the cleansing
outflow of your soul.

ENDINGS

Will I accept the death that waits
'til time is up, and sup instead
on joys and pleasure of the life I've led?

Probably I will, for dreaming up
a pain or misery I can't foresee is
such a waste of brain.

I'd rather stay just as I am and let
the Powers that Be create a brand
new life for me to love again.

Marjorie J. Scott

A PLEA BEFORE I LEAVE

I am not myself, I am also you,
the tree of your life as well as my own,
beckoning, binding, blessing.

Beyond the limits of your consciousness
we exist as floating particles in the
cosmic soup, you share, you care,
often unaware of our abundant unity
before this millennium, the separation
of centuries gone by so filled with
pain, you have considered self
destruction as the only pacifier.

Within your spirit enduring, persisting,
let confronting truth call on your will,
keep you prayerfully alert to how
humankind has been duped and
scammed (however well-meaning in
the crime) by awesome intellects of
the past four centuries, bent on being
pundits, idols, lord-like leaders.

Now, instead of "I am all alone",
join in the heaven-sent shout
"we truly are ALL ONE!"

ABOUT THE AUTHOR

Marjorie J. Scott "published" her first piece, a one-act play, in 2nd grade. She's been writing ever since: from school newspapers to ad agency copywriter and community newspaper editor. Now retired, she concentrates on opinion pieces, and poetry of which she says, "Poems write *me*." Several have won first and second prizes in competitions sponsored by National League of American Penwomen, of which she was a member.